Follow Your

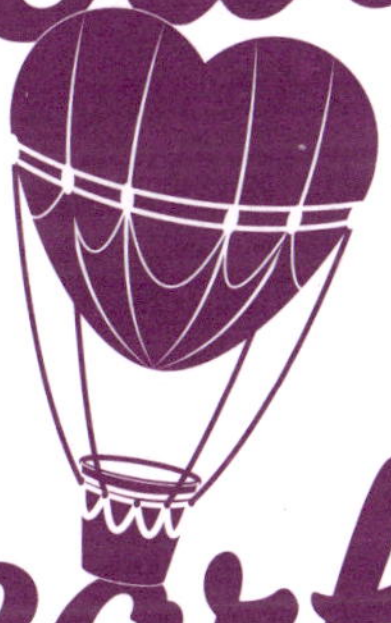

Heart

Published 2024

FiNGERPRINT!

An imprint of Prakash Books India Pvt. Ltd

113/A, Darya Ganj,
New Delhi-110 002
Email: info@prakashbooks.com/sales@prakashbooks.com

 Fingerprint Publishing
 @FingerprintP
 @fingerprintpublishingbooks
www.fingerprintpublishing.com

ISBN: 978 93 5856 222 4

To . . . .

From . . . .

The fight between the head and the heart is a tale as old as time. Amidst the trappings of a monotonous life, we all have a voice inside our heads asking us to do that one thing that truly expresses who we are and gives us happiness!

But what is stopping us? The fear of failure and pushback? But isn't failure far better than answering all those "what ifs" down the road?

So, you can either adjust and chip away at your passion to fit into the mold of society, or pursue your curiosities, interests, and love. So, in the journey of life, take the driver's seat and . . . Follow Your Heart!

"ONE PERSON WITH
PASSION IS BETTER
THAN FORTY PEOPLE
MERELY INTERESTED."

E. M. FORSTER

"BEING DEEPLY LOVED
BY SOMEONE GIVES
YOU STRENGTH, WHILE
LOVING SOMEONE DEEPLY
GIVES YOU COURAGE."

Lao Tzu

"Nobody has ever measured,
even the poets, how much
heart can hold."

ZELDA FITZGERALD

"NEVER LET THE FEAR
OF STRIKING OUT KEEP YOU
FROM PLAYING THE GAME."

BABE RUTH

"DO NOT GO WHERE THE PATH MAY LEAD, GO INSTEAD WHERE THERE IS NO PATH AND LEAVE A TRAIL."

RALPH WALDO EMERSON

"If you want to be successful
in this world, you have
to follow your passion,
not your paycheck."

ANONYMOUS

"I have no special talents.
I am only passionately curious."

ALBERT EINSTEIN

"NO ONE HAS EVER
ACHIEVED ANYTHING
FROM THE SMALLEST
TO THE GREATEST
UNLESS THE DREAM
WAS DREAMED FIRST."

Laura Ingalls Wilder

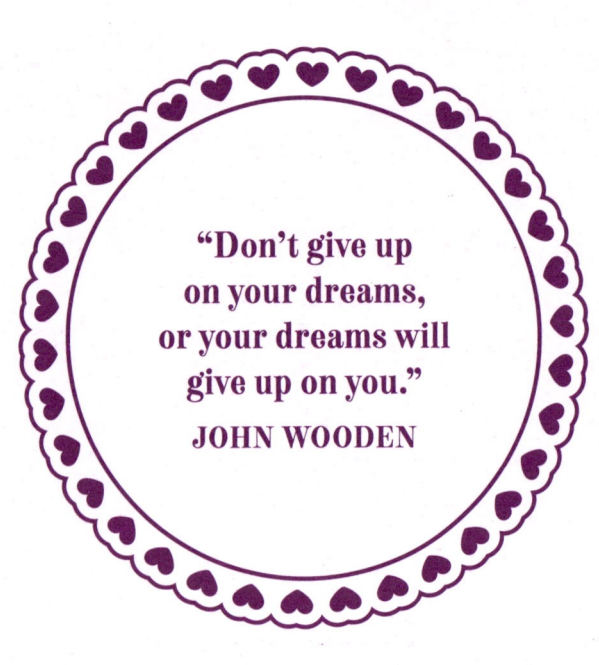

"Don't give up
on your dreams,
or your dreams will
give up on you."

JOHN WOODEN

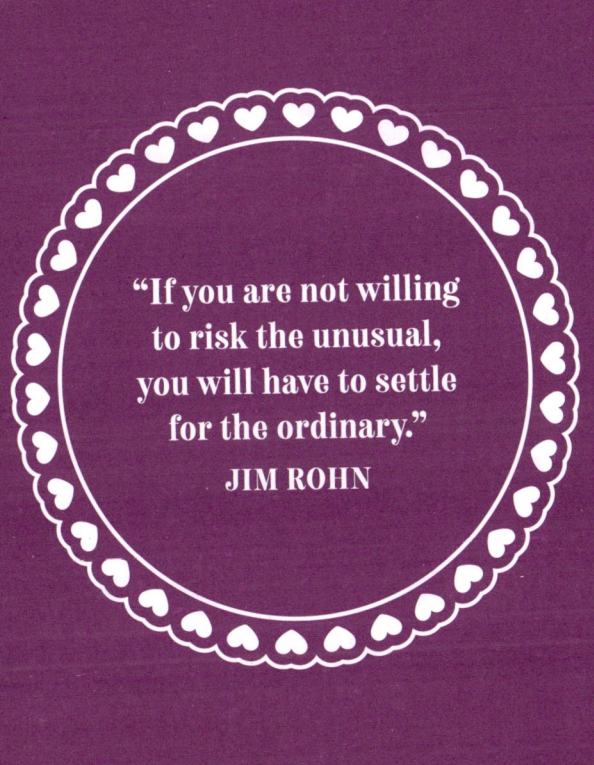

"If you are not willing
to risk the unusual,
you will have to settle
for the ordinary."

JIM ROHN

"There are no rules.
Just follow your heart."

**ROBIN
WILLIAMS**

"Seek freedom and become captive of your desires. Seek discipline and find your liberty."

FRANK HERBERT

"Keep your feet on the ground, but let your heart soar as high as it will. Refuse to be average or to surrender to the chill of your spiritual environment."

ARTHUR HELPS

"I prefer to be a dreamer among the humblest, with visions to be realized, than lord among those without dreams and desires."

KHALIL
GIBRAN

"Dare to dream, but
even more importantly,
dare to put action
behind your dreams."

JOSH HINDS

"Dream as if you'll live forever, live as if you'll die today."

JAMES DEAN

"Life is inherently risky. There is only one big risk you should avoid at all costs, and that is the risk of doing nothing."

DENIS WAITLEY

"Don't let small minds
convince you that your
dreams are too big."

ANONYMOUS

"ONLY THOSE WHO WILL
RISK GOING TOO FAR
CAN POSSIBLY FIND OUT
HOW FAR ONE CAN GO."

T. S. Eliot

"EVERY MAN DIES, BUT NOT EVERY MAN REALLY LIVES."

WILLIAM WALLACE

"THE BEST AND MOST BEAUTIFUL
THINGS IN THE WORLD CANNOT
BE SEEN OR EVEN TOUCHED —THEY
MUST BE FELT WITH THE HEART."

HELEN KELLER

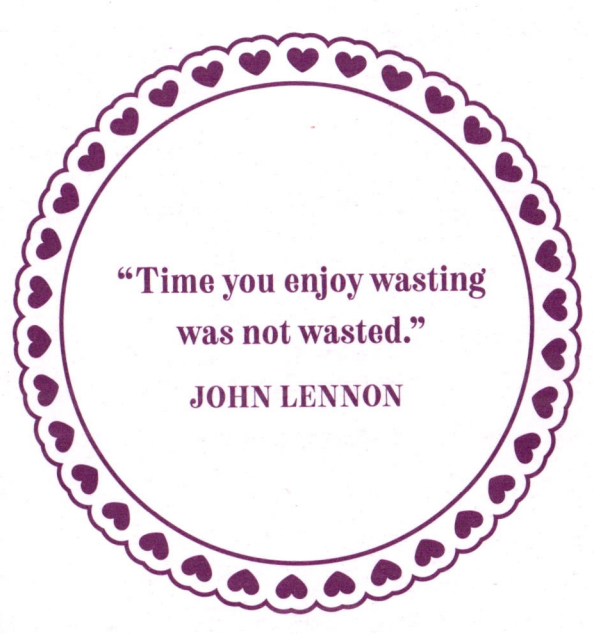

"Time you enjoy wasting
was not wasted."

JOHN LENNON

"LIFE IS GOING TO GIVE
YOU JUST WHAT YOU PUT
IN IT. PUT YOUR WHOLE
HEART IN EVERYTHING
YOU DO, AND PRAY,
THEN YOU CAN WAIT."

Maya Angelou

"YOU HAVE TO DREAM BEFORE YOUR DREAMS CAN COME TRUE."

A. P. J. ABDUL KALAM

"He who reigns within himself and rules passions, desires, and fears is more than a king."

JOHN MILTON

"He who desires,
but acts not,
breeds pestilence."

**WILLIAM
BLAKE**

"Passion is in all great
searches and is necessary
to all creative endeavors."

W. EUGENE SMITH

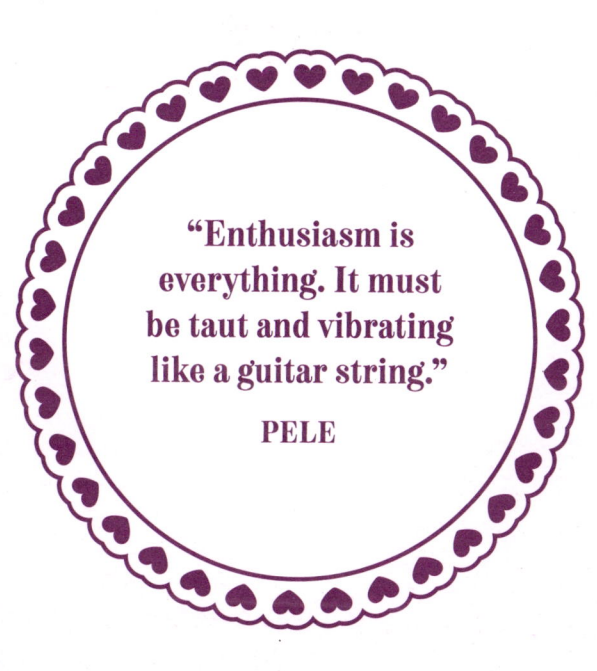

"Enthusiasm is
everything. It must
be taut and vibrating
like a guitar string."

PELE

"I have to face life with a newly found passion. I must rediscover the irresistible will to learn, to live and to love."

ANDREA BOCELLI

"Don't wait.
Life goes faster
than you think."

ANONYMOUS

"I firmly believe that any man's finest hour, the greatest fulfillment of all that he holds dear, is that moment when he has worked his heart out in a good cause and lies exhausted on the field of battle—victorious."

VINCE LOMBARDI

"There is not love
where there is no will."

**INDIRA
GANDHI**

"Let yourself be silently drawn by the strange pull of what you really love. It will not lead you astray."

RUMI

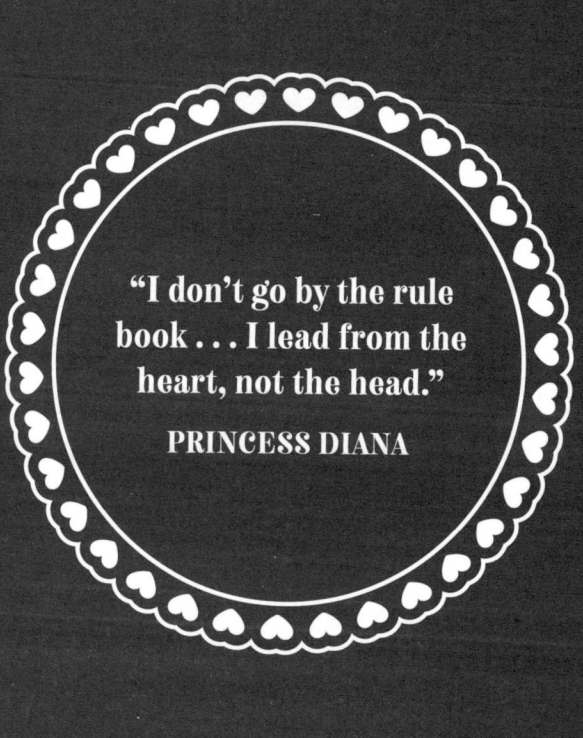

"I don't go by the rule book . . . I lead from the heart, not the head."

PRINCESS DIANA

"YOU WILL NEVER FOLLOW
YOUR OWN INNER VOICE
UNTIL YOU CLEAR UP THE
DOUBTS IN YOUR MIND."

Roy T. Bennett

"Wherever you go,
go with all your heart."

CONFUCIUS

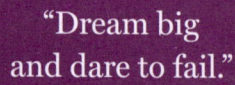

"Dream big
and dare to fail."

**NORMAN
VAUGHAN**

"No profit grows where is no pleasure ta'en"

WILLIAM SHAKESPEARE

"IF YOU ALWAYS
DO WHAT INTERESTS
YOU, AT LEAST ONE
PERSON IS PLEASED."

Katharine Hepburn

"To succeed you have to believe
in something with such passion
that it becomes a reality."

ANITA RODDICK

"Nothing great in the world has ever been accomplished without passion."

GEORG HEGEL

"DON'T GO INTO SOMETHING TO TEST THE WATERS, GO INTO THINGS TO MAKE WAVES."

ANONYMOUS

"Passion will move men beyond themselves, beyond their shortcomings, beyond their failures."

JOSEPH CAMPBELL

"Love life, engage in it,
give it all you've got.
Love it with a passion,
because life truly does give
back, many times over,
what you put into it."

MAYA ANGELOU

"Always remember, you
have within you the
strength, the patience, and
the passion to reach for the
star to change the world."

HARRIET TUBMAN

"If you don't love what you
do, you won't do it with much
conviction or passion."

MIA HAMM

"NOTHING IS AS
IMPORTANT AS PASSION.
NO MATTER WHAT YOU
WANT TO DO WITH YOUR
LIFE, BE PASSIONATE."

Jon Bon Jovi

People Who Followed Their Heart and Made A Difference! ♥

♥ A simple girl from Louisiana sold vacuum cleaners door-to-door, worked as a paralegal doing clerical work for a law company, and shucked oysters before following her passion of becoming an entertainer. Now, she is a well-known comedian and had her own talk show, The **Ellen DeGeneres** Show.

♥ Did you know that **Walt Disney** served as a hospital driver in France during World War I? He next worked as an editor for a newspaper but was let go because he "lacked imagination" and "had no decent ideas." Criticized by all, he is now counted among the best cartoonists of all time because, regardless of all the setbacks, he followed his passion of making a cartoon series!

- **Brandon Stanton** moved from Chicago to New York in 2010. A mere self-taught photographer who had recently ended a brief career in bond trading set out to capture 10,000 individuals on the streets of New York City and create a blog! For the first year, it was largely disregarded, but now, that blog is known as, Humans of New York, which is incredibly famous and has helped Stanton land a few book deals.

- **J.K. Rowling**, the creator of the Harry Potter fiction series, began her career with Amnesty International as a researcher and bilingual secretary. She lived in poverty after losing her job but never lost her passion for writing! Despite lack of resources, she followed her heart and is now recognized as the first individual to earn a billion dollars from writing books.

"Don't be too timid
and squeamish
about your actions.
All life is an experiment.
The more experiments
you make the better."

RALPH WALDO EMERSON

"JUST DON'T GIVE UP TRYING TO
DO WHAT YOU REALLY WANT TO DO.
WHERE THERE IS LOVE AND
INSPIRATION, I DON'T THINK
YOU CAN GO WRONG."

ELLA FITZGERALD

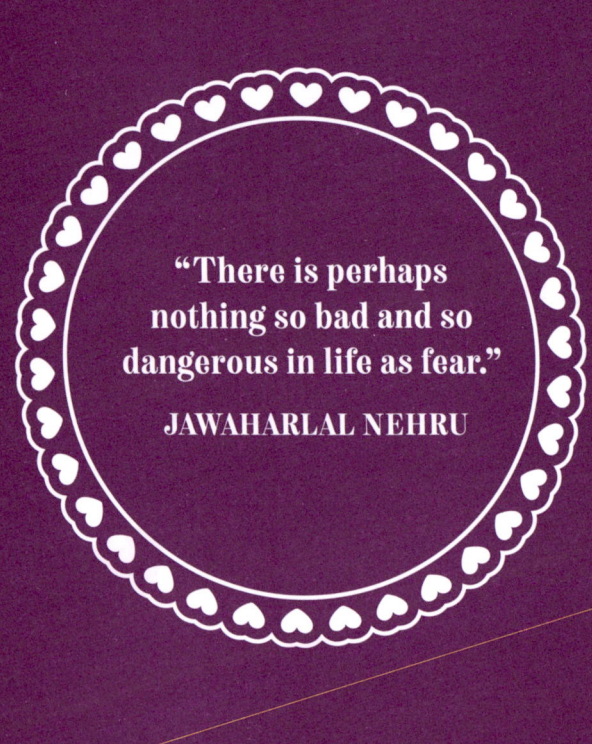

"There is perhaps nothing so bad and so dangerous in life as fear."

JAWAHARLAL NEHRU

"There is no passion
to be found playing
small—in settling for a life
that is less than the one
you are capable of living."

NELSON MANDELA

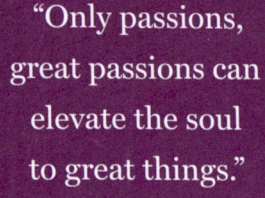

"Only passions,
great passions can
elevate the soul
to great things."

**DENIS
DIDEROT**

"Great dancers are not great
because of their technique,
they are great because
of their passion."

**MARTHA
GRAHAM**

"There is a wisdom
of the head and
wisdom of the heart."

CHARLES DICKENS

"EVERY MORNING YOU HAVE
TWO CHOICES: CONTINUE
TO SLEEP WITH YOU DREAMS,
OR WAKE UP AND CHASE THEM."

ANONYMOUS

"There is scarcely any passion without struggle."

ALBERT CAMUS

"I want to know what passion is. I want to feel something strongly."

ALDOUS HUXLEY

"INTELLECTUAL PASSION DRIVES OUT SENSUALITY."

LEONARDO DA VINCI

"CLARITY OF MIND
MEANS CLARITY OF
PASSION TOO; THIS IS
WHY A GREAT AND CLEAR
MIND LOVES ARDENTLY
AND SEES DISTINCTLY
WHAT IT LOVES."

Blaise Pascal

"Paradise is to love many
things with a passion."

PABLO PICASSO

"Make mistakes, take chances, be silly, be imperfect, trust yourself and follow your heart."

ANONYMOUS

"A goal is a dream
with a deadline."

NAPOLEON HILL

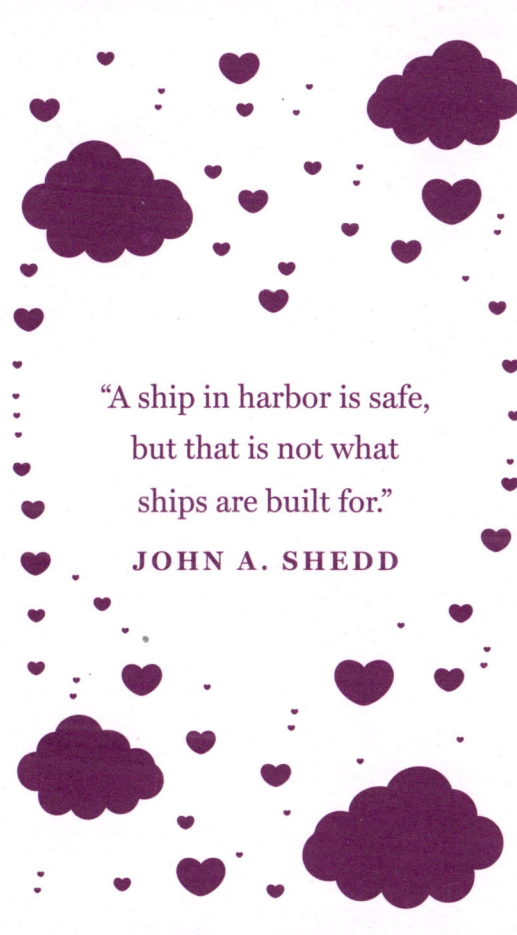

"A ship in harbor is safe,
but that is not what
ships are built for."

JOHN A. SHEDD

"Follow your own passion—not your parents', not your teachers'—yours."

ROBERT BALLARD

"I am seeking, I am striving,
I am in it with all my heart."

**VINCENT
VAN GOGH**

"THE VERY BASIC OF A MAN'S
LIVING SPIRIT IS HIS PASSION
FOR ADVENTURE."

CHRISTOPHER MCCANDLESS

"Anything that gets your blood racing is probably worth doing."

HUNTER S. THOMPSON

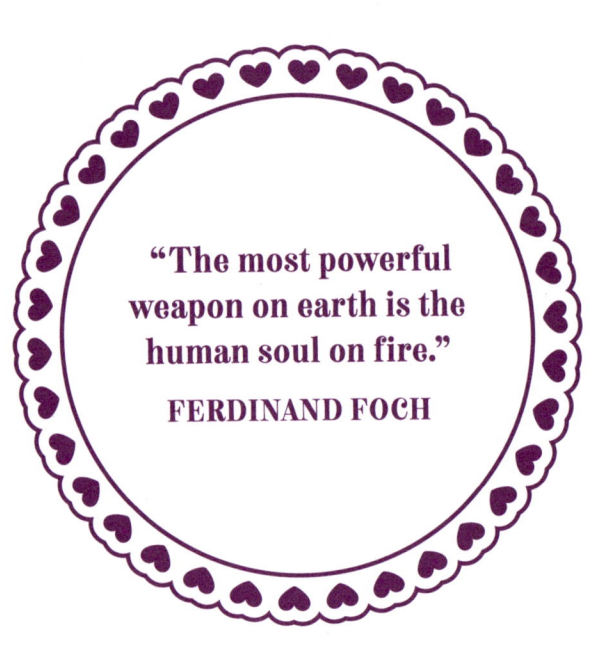

"The most powerful weapon on earth is the human soul on fire."

FERDINAND FOCH

"I'VE BEEN ABSOLUTELY
TERRIFIED EVERY
MOMENT OF MY LIFE
AND I'VE NEVER LET IT
KEEP ME FROM DOING
A SINGLE THING THAT
I WANTED TO DO."

Georgia O'Keeffe

"Our passion for learning
. . . is our tool for survival."

CARL SAGAN

"Sometimes life is about risking everything for a dream no one can see but you."

ANONYMOUS

"What to ourselves
in passion we propose,
The passion ending,
doth the purpose lose."

**WILLIAM
SHAKESPEARE**

"DON'T BE AFRAID TO BE AFRAID."

MAURICE CHEVALIER

"Follow your heart.
Do what you love.
Because I was constantly
struggling with that.
If it's in your heart, go for it.
Don't listen to other people."

MAZ JOBRANI

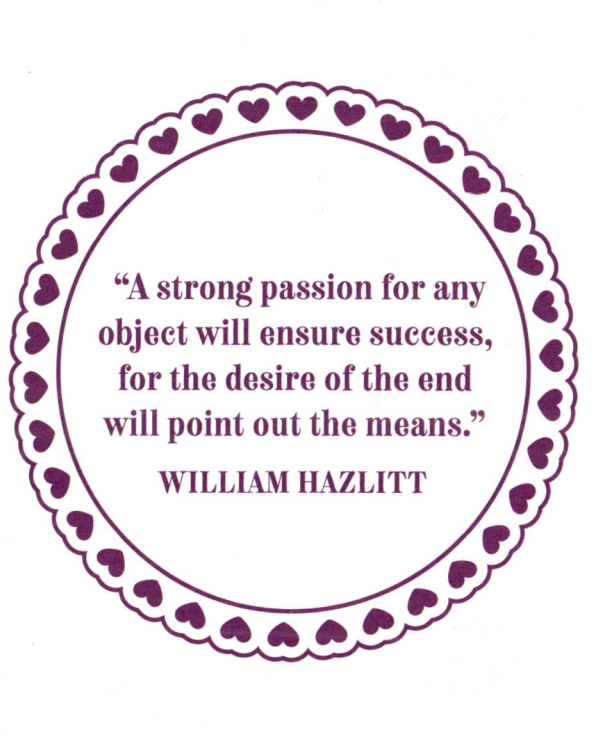

"A strong passion for any object will ensure success, for the desire of the end will point out the means."

WILLIAM HAZLITT

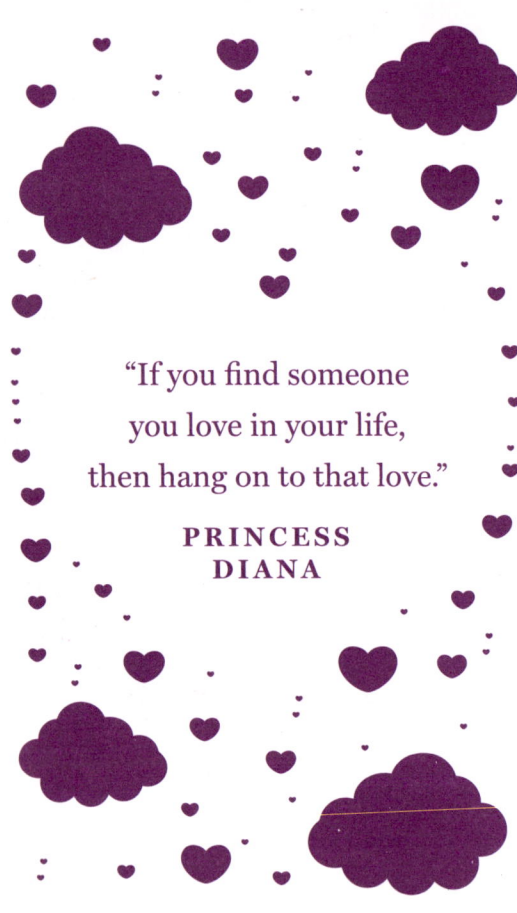

"If you find someone
you love in your life,
then hang on to that love."

**PRINCESS
DIANA**

"Enthusiasm brushes off
upon those with whom
you come in contact."

**JOHN
WOODEN**

"ACTION IS THE
FOUNDATIONAL KEY
TO ALL SUCCESS."

Pablo Picasso

"A dream doesn't become reality through magic; it takes sweat, determination and hard work."

COLIN POWELL

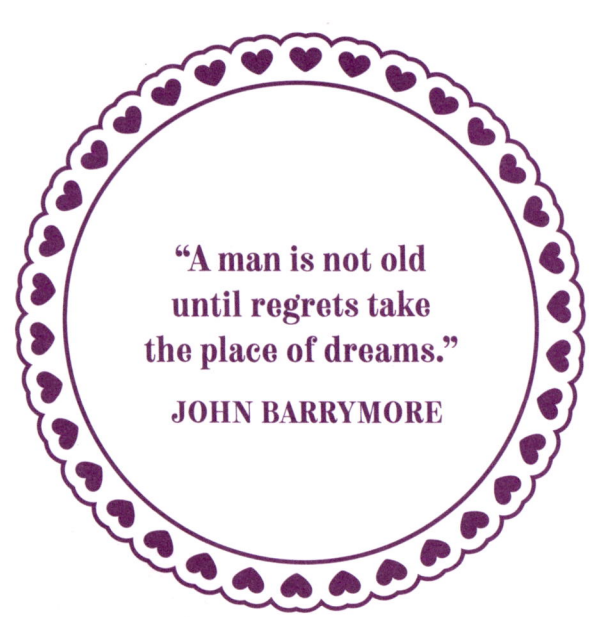

"A man is not old
until regrets take
the place of dreams."

JOHN BARRYMORE

"Don't tell people
your dreams.
Show them."

ANONYMOUS

"All our dreams can come true, if we have the courage to pursue them."

WALT DISNEY

"As soon as you start to pursue a dream, your life wakes up and everything has meaning."

BARBARA SHER

"BELIEVE YOU CAN AND YOU'RE HALFWAY THERE."

THEODORE ROOSEVELT

"BREATHING DREAMS
LIKE AIR."

F. Scott Fitzgerald

"Knowledge of mankind is knowledge of their passions."

BENJAMIN DISRAELI

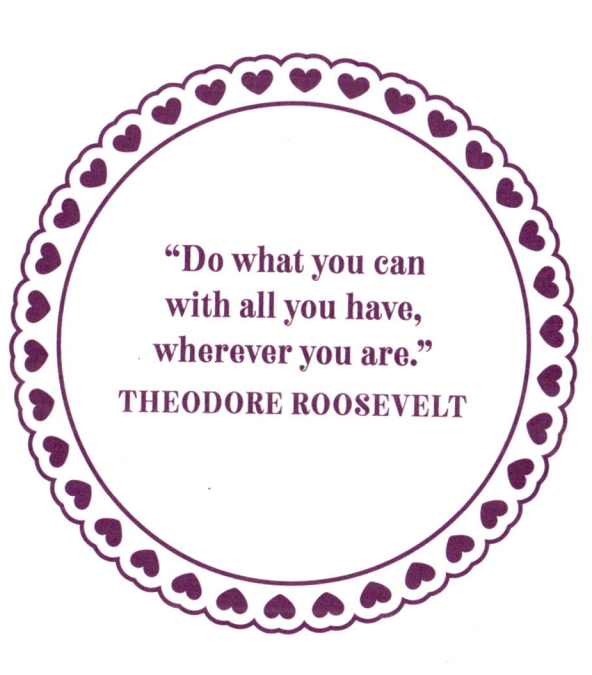

"Do what you can
with all you have,
wherever you are."

THEODORE ROOSEVELT

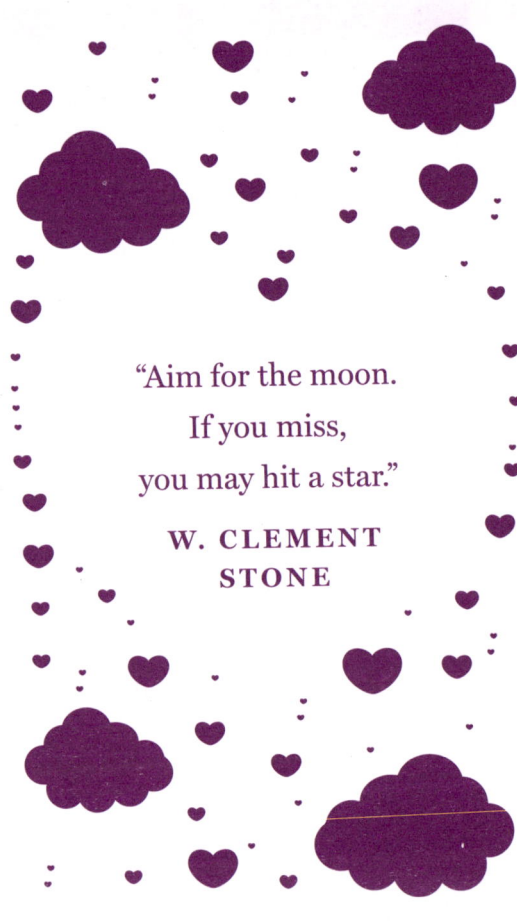

"Aim for the moon.
If you miss,
you may hit a star."

**W. CLEMENT
STONE**

"Dream no small dreams
for they have no power to
move the hearts of men."

GOETHE

"Dreams are today's answers
to tomorrow's questions."

EDGAR CAYCE

"NEVER GIVE UP ON A DREAM
JUST BECAUSE OF THE TIME IT
WILL TAKE TO ACCOMPLISH IT.
THE TIME WILL PASS ANYWAY."

EARL NIGHTINGALE

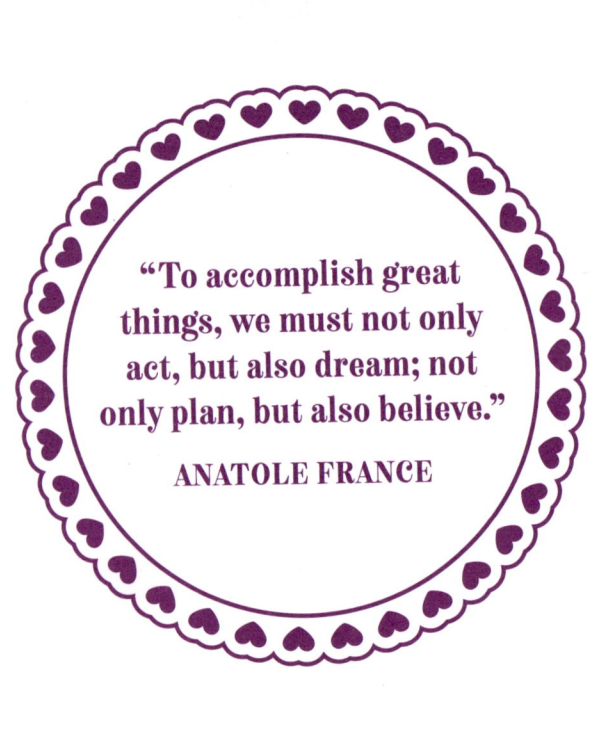

"To accomplish great
things, we must not only
act, but also dream; not
only plan, but also believe."

ANATOLE FRANCE

"SO MANY OF OUR
DREAMS AT FIRST SEEM
IMPOSSIBLE, THEN THEY
SEEM IMPROBABLE, AND
THEN, WHEN WE SUMMON
THE WILL, THEY SOON
BECOME INEVITABLE."

Christopher Reeve

"Fall seven times
and stand up eight."

ANONYMOUS

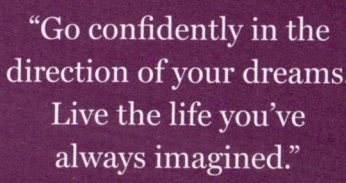

"Go confidently in the
direction of your dreams.
Live the life you've
always imagined."

**HENRY DAVID
THOREAU**

"Hope lies
in dreams, in
imagination, and in
the courage of those
who dare to make
dreams into reality."

JONAS SALK

"Hold fast to dreams,
for if dreams die,
life is a broken-winged
bird that cannot fly."

LANGSTON HUGHES

"I have not failed,
I have just found
10,000 ways that
won't work."

**THOMAS A.
EDISON**

"I WOULD RATHER
DIE OF PASSION
THAN OF BOREDOM."

Vincent Van Gogh

"Chase your passion,
not your pension."

DENIS WAITLEY

"Others may have more
ability than you, they may
be larger, faster, quicker, better
jumpers . . . but no one should
be your superior in respect to
team spirit, loyalty, enthusiasm,
cooperation, determination,
industriousness, fight,
effort, and character."

JOHN WOODEN

How to Follow Your Heart?

- ♥ It's all about taking risks! You will never know what you are capable of if you never give it a try.

- ♥ Reflect on your interests. Sometimes, we are so caught with the mundane, we lose our hobbies. Make a list of your hobbies and try to get back to them.

- ♥ Be curious and always eager to learn.

- ♥ Be consistent and don't be disheartened by failures. You can have the biggest dreams in the world, but unless you take action to make them a reality, they will remain dreams.

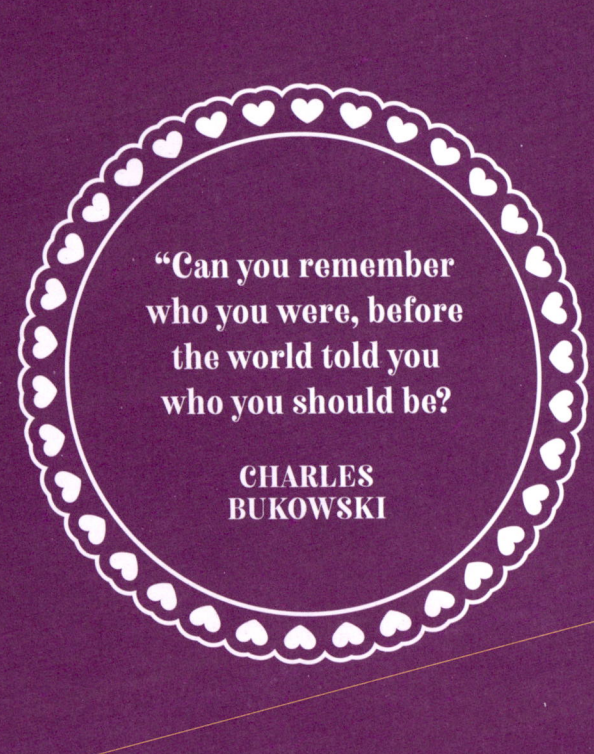

"Can you remember
who you were, before
the world told you
who you should be?

CHARLES
BUKOWSKI

"The ones who are crazy enough
to think they can change the
world are the ones that do."

**STEVE
JOBS**

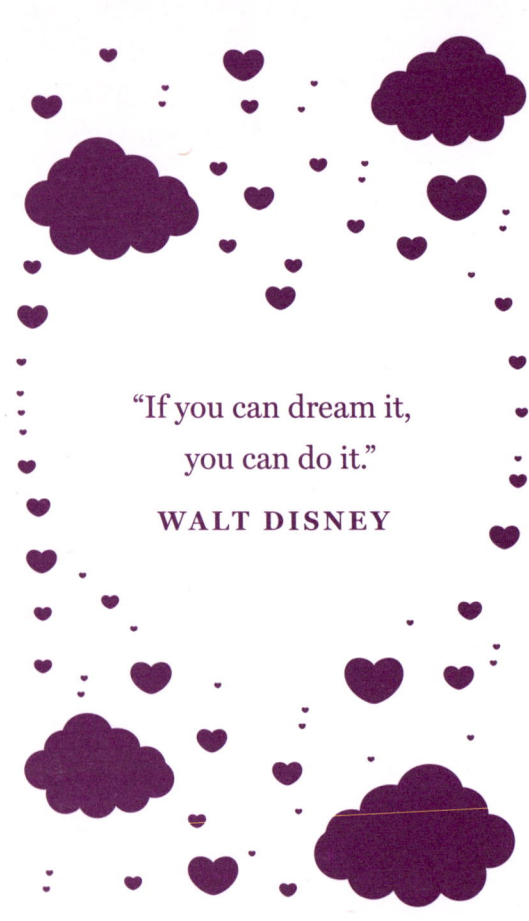

"If you can dream it,
you can do it."

WALT DISNEY

"If you feel like there's something out there that you're supposed to be doing, if you have a passion for it, then stop wishing and just do it."

WANDA SYKES

"Without passion man is a mere latent force and possibility, like the flint which awaits the shock of the iron before it can give forth its spark."

HENRI-FRÉDÉRIC AMIEL

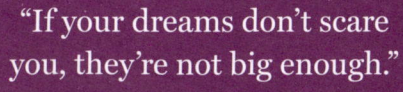

"If your dreams don't scare you, they're not big enough."

MUHAMMAD ALI

**"IT IS NEVER TOO LATE TO BE
WHAT YOU MIGHT HAVE BEEN."**

GEORGE ELIOT

"IT MAY BE THAT
THOSE WHO DO
MOST, DREAM MOST."

Stephen Butler Leacock

"Follow your heart.
Life is too short
to be sidetracked
by things everyone
else wants you to do."

ANONYMOUS

"Love what you do
and do what you love.
Don't listen to anyone else
who tells you not to do it.
You do what you want, what
you love. Imagination should
be the center of your life."

RAY BRADBURY

"Never give up on what
you really want to do.
The person with big dreams
is more powerful than the
one with all the facts."

ALBERT EINSTEIN

"Man, alone, has the power
to transform his thoughts into
physical reality; man, alone,
can dream and make
his dreams come true."

NAPOLEON HILL

"FAR AND AWAY THE BEST PRIZE THAT
LIFE OFFERS IS THE CHANCE TO WORK
HARD AT WORK WORTH DOING."

THEODORE ROOSEVELT

"WHEN I LET GO
OF WHAT I AM,
I BECOME WHAT
I MIGHT BE."

Lao Tzu

"Nothing happens
unless first we dream."

CARL SANDBURG

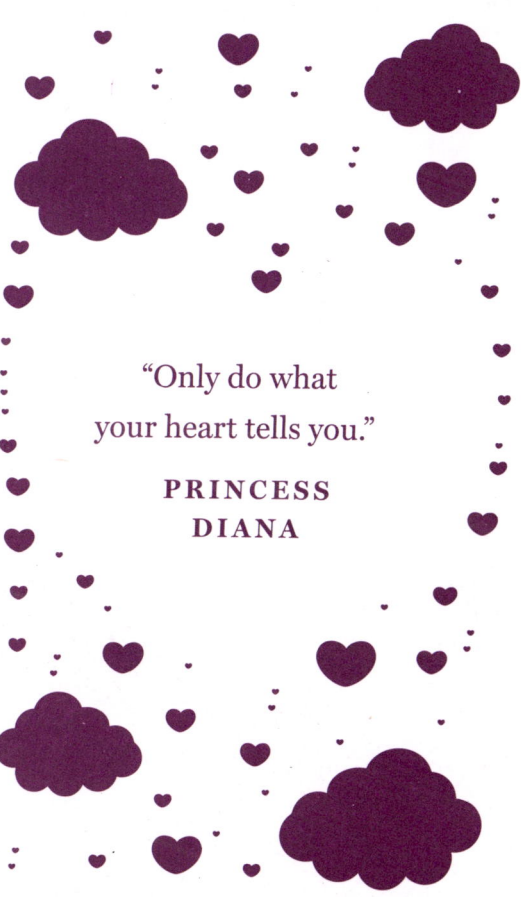

"Only do what
your heart tells you."

**PRINCESS
DIANA**

"Passion is energy. Feel the power that comes from focusing on what excites you."

OPRAH WINFREY

"Only put off until tomorrow what you are willing to die having left undone."

PABLO PICASSO

"CHASE DOWN YOUR
PASSION LIKE IT'S THE
LAST BUS OF THE NIGHT."

TERRI GUILLEMETS

"Imagination
is more important
than knowledge."

ALBERT EINSTEIN

"If it's both terrifying and amazing then you should definitely pursue it."

ANONYMOUS

"EVERYTHING YOU CAN
IMAGINE IS REAL."

Pablo Picasso

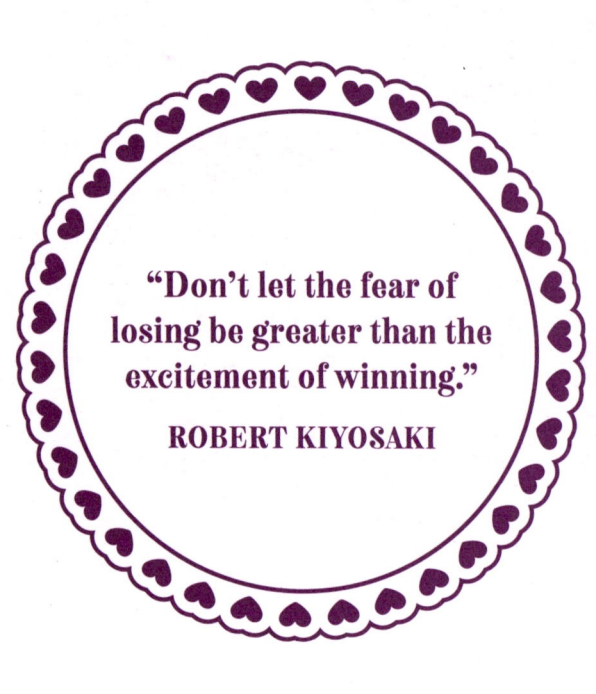

"Don't let the fear of losing be greater than the excitement of winning."

ROBERT KIYOSAKI

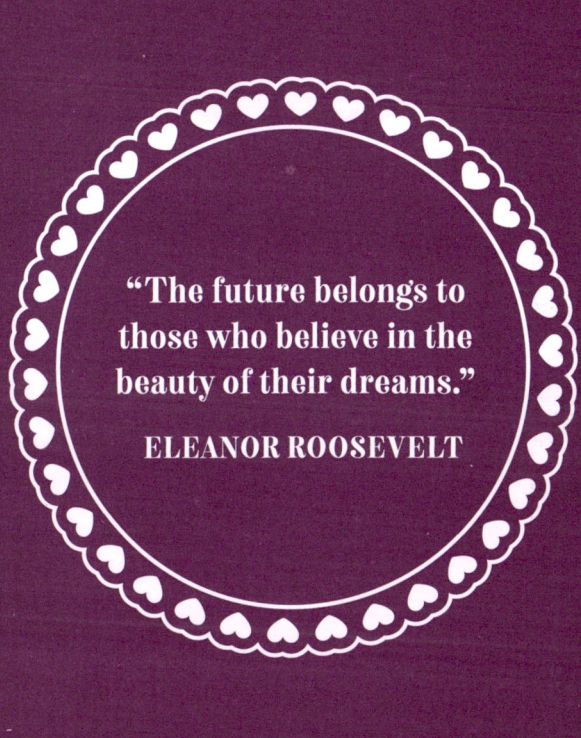

"The future belongs to those who believe in the beauty of their dreams."

ELEANOR ROOSEVELT

"Once we believe in ourselves, we can risk curiosity, wonder, spontaneous delight, or any experiences that reveal the human spirit."

E.E. CUMMINGS

"All that was great in the past was ridiculed, condemned, combated, suppressed–only to emerge all the more powerfully, all the more triumphantly from the struggle."

NIKOLA TESLA

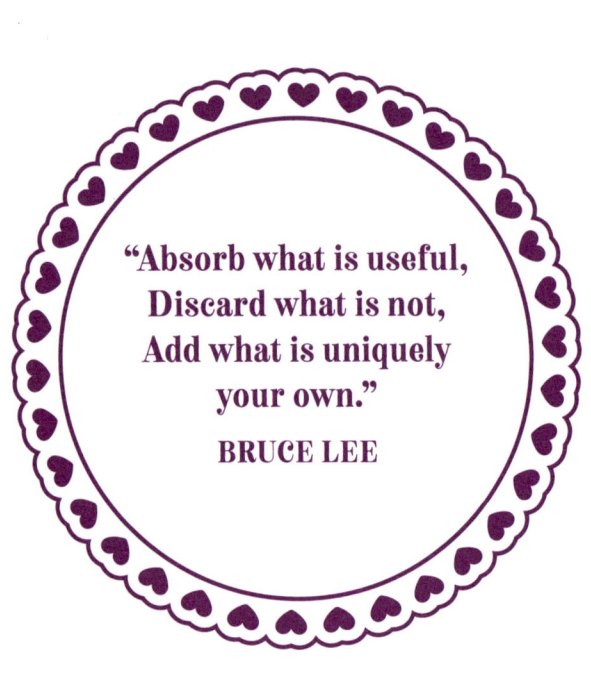

"Absorb what is useful,
Discard what is not,
Add what is uniquely
your own."

BRUCE LEE

"Follow your honest convictions, and stay strong."

WILLIAM THACKERAY

"YOU ARE NEVER TOO
OLD TO SET ANOTHER
GOAL OR TO DREAM
A NEW DREAM."

C.S. Lewis

"I LIKE TO BE A FREE SPIRIT.
SOME DON'T LIKE THAT,
BUT THAT'S THE WAY I AM."

PRINCESS DIANA

"To be a human being is to be in a state of tension between your appetites and your dreams, and the social realities around you and your obligations to your fellow man."

JOHN UPDIKE

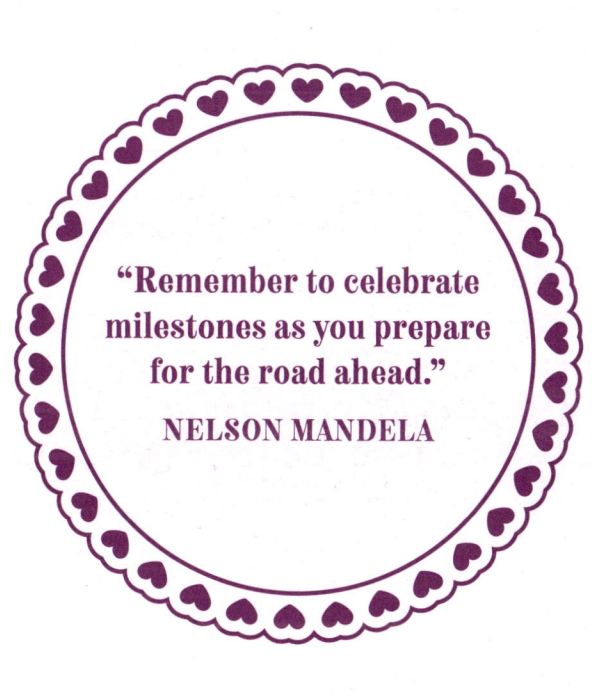

"Remember to celebrate milestones as you prepare for the road ahead."

NELSON MANDELA

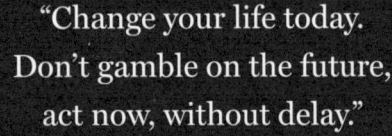

"Change your life today.
Don't gamble on the future,
act now, without delay."

**SIMONE
DE BEAUVOIR**

"Life isn't about finding yourself. Life is about creating yourself."

GEORGE BERNARD SHAW

"My mission in life is not merely to survive, but to thrive; and to do so with some passion, some compassion, some humor, and some style."

MAYA ANGELOU

"A GREAT LEADER'S COURAGE TO FULFILL HIS VISION COMES FROM PASSION, NOT POSITION."

JOHN C. MAXWELL

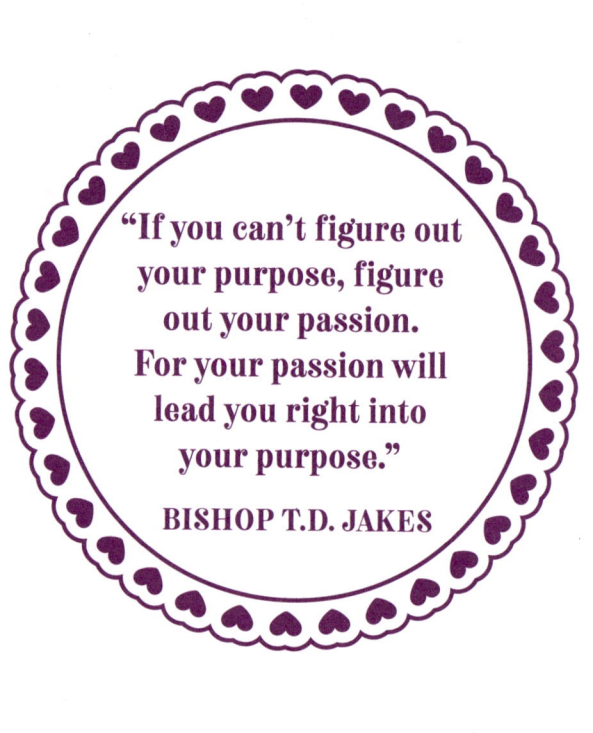

"If you can't figure out your purpose, figure out your passion. For your passion will lead you right into your purpose."

BISHOP T.D. JAKES

"Stop dreaming about your bucket list and start living it."

ANNETTE WHITE

"Don't think too much, you'll think your whole life away. Just stop, close your eyes, and follow your heart. I guarantee you, it knows the way."

ANONYMOUS

"YOU CAN DO ANYTHING
AS LONG AS YOU HAVE
THE PASSION, THE DRIVE,
THE FOCUS, AND THE SUPPORT."

SABRINA BRYAN

"Follow your heart, and listen when it speaks to you. The answers you seek are within its words."

MICHELLE C. USTASZEWSKI

"THE HEART'S INTUITIVE INTELLIGENCE IS THE PATH TO HEALING AND A FULFILLING LIFE."

ROLLIN MCCRATY

"EVERYTHING YOU'VE
EVER WANTED IS ON THE
OTHER SIDE OF FEAR."

GEORGE ADDAIR